The Rushed Gourmet H

Profes:

## Casimir Thistledown

*"Why rush through life when you can saunter through it, one decadent dish at a time? Bon appétit!"*

Copyright © 2023  Casimir Thistledown
All rights reserved

Introduction
Author's Note: Embarking on a Gourmet Odyssey
Chapter 1: The Essentials of Gourmet Dining
Chapter 2: The Busy Professional's Kitchen
Chapter 3: Mastering the Basics
Chapter 4: The Gourmet Pantry
Chapter 5: From Quick Bites to Culinary Feats
Chapter 6: The Art of Menu Planning
Chapter 7: Savory Secrets for Busy Professionals
Chapter 8: Effortless Elegance
Chapter 9: Dining Out Like a Pro
Chapter 10: Hosting Impromptu Gatherings
Chapter 11: Travelling the World through Your Plate
Recipes
Conclusion
Culinary Glossary
Recommended Resources for Gourmet Fine Dining
Afterword: Reflecting on Gourmet Dining

# Introduction

Ah, my dearest connoisseurs of the hurried life, permit me to extend the most refined of welcomes to the enchanting realm of "**The Rushed Gourmet Handbook for Busy Professionals.**"

Within these elegant pages, we shall embark on a voyage that is nothing short of culinary brilliance amidst the relentless whirlwind of our modern lives.

Imagine yourself, if you will, as the contemporary virtuoso, an artist of multitasking, able to conjure culinary magic amid the tumultuous orchestra of meetings, appointments, and conference calls.

While the world clamours for our attention, we shall serenely dine in decadence, forgoing compromise and embracing taste with an unwavering resolve.

In this hasty age of ringing phones, ceaseless emails, and deadlines that loom like dark clouds, we shall find sanctuary in the comforting embrace of a well-crafted dish.

Armed with wit as sharp as a chef's knife and humour as delightful as the pop of a champagne cork, we shall navigate this culinary odyssey together.

Ladies and gentlemen, cinch your aprons with the elegance of a bowtie, sharpen your senses like the keenest of knives, and prepare to relish the epicurean treasures that lie ahead.

Within these pages, we shall not merely endure the rush; we shall savour it, and do so with all the sophistication of the most discerning epicurean on the planet.

Bon appétit!

## Author's Note: Embarking on a Gourmet Odyssey

My dear readers, as we step further into the enchanting world of "The Rushed Gourmet Handbook for Busy Professionals," I felt it only fitting to share a few words—a veritable appetiser, if you will.

The journey we're about to undertake is nothing short of epic, and I want you to be well-prepared for the gastronomic odyssey that awaits.

### In the Wake of Our Culinary Overture

In our introduction, we dipped our toes into the delectable pool of "The Rushed Gourmet" lifestyle, where culinary excellence meets the hustle and bustle of the modern professional.

We embraced the notion that you can be a maestro in the office and a virtuoso in the kitchen. But here, in this author's note, I'd like to dive deeper into the purpose of this culinary voyage.

### Why "The Rushed Gourmet"?

Why, indeed! An excellent question. You might wonder why such a handbook is necessary in a world of takeout and fast-food frenzy. Well, my discerning reader, it's precisely because of the "rush" that we find ourselves in need of gourmet guidance.

In our harried lives, where deadlines loom larger than soufflés and meetings outnumber macarons, the need for a culinary compass has never been more apparent.

"The Rushed Gourmet" is your North Star in a constellation of culinary chaos, guiding you through the gastronomic galaxy with grace and gusto.

## A Culinary Symphony in the Making

As we move forward, allow me to promise you this: You'll find no pretentious platitudes here. Instead, expect a whimsical waltz through the world of fine flavours, a tango with time-saving techniques, and a sonnet of shortcuts for the discerning diner.

This handbook is a journey of culinary self-discovery. It's a passport to the realms of taste, where you'll explore the art of fine dining and ultimately transform into the culinary genius you were born to be.

## A Toast to Adventure

So, raise your metaphorical goblets, my friends, to the adventures that lie ahead. Whether you're a novice in the kitchen or a seasoned sous-chef, together, we shall navigate the path of the Rushed Gourmet, adding a pinch of wit and a dash of humour, to our culinary creations.

With enthusiasm in my heart and a chef's hat atop my head, I invite you to embark on this epicurean journey. It's time to don your apron, sharpen your knives, and prepare to conquer the culinary world—one delicious recipe at a time.

Bon appétit with a side of audacity,

Casimir Thistledown, Your Culinary Captain and Maestro of Mirth

# **Chapter 1: The Essentials of Gourmet Dining**

In the realm of culinary pleasures, there exists a pinnacle of gastronomic delight known as Fine Dining.

It's more than a meal; it's a symphony of flavours, a carefully choreographed ballet of textures, and an artful presentation that engages all your senses.

Fine dining is an exquisite journey that demands appreciation and understanding of its nuances.

In this chapter, we embark on a voyage through the heart of gourmet dining, unravelling the secrets and principles that elevate a meal into an unforgettable experience.

As we delve into "**The Essentials of Gourmet Dining**," we will explore three fundamental aspects that define this world of culinary excellence.

We will unveil the artistry behind fine dining, providing profound insights into the ambiance, etiquette, and atmosphere that set the stage.

We will guide you in elevating your taste buds, encouraging a deeper appreciation for the intricacies of flavours, textures, and sensory experiences.

Lastly, we will examine the vital role of presentation, where each plate becomes a canvas, and every dish an edible masterpiece.

Prepare to be enlightened, as we embark on a journey that will not only tantalise your taste buds but also enrich your understanding of the culinary arts.

Welcome to the world of gourmet dining, where every meal is a celebration of taste, culture, and craftsmanship.

- **The Art of Fine Dining Unveiled**

Fine Dining is a culinary experience that goes beyond mere sustenance; it's an art form. To truly appreciate it, consider these aspects:

**Ambiance**: The atmosphere is crucial. Fine dining restaurants often feature elegant decor, soft lighting, and soothing music to create a sophisticated environment.

**Reservations**: Plan ahead and make reservations. Fine dining establishments tend to be popular and fill up quickly.

**Dress Code**: Dress appropriately. Most fine dining restaurants have a dress code, which may include wearing formal attire.

**Etiquette**: Familiarise yourself with dining etiquette. This includes using utensils correctly, knowing when to start eating, and engaging in polite conversation.

**Menu Exploration**: Be adventurous with your palate. Explore the menu, and don't hesitate to ask the waiter for recommendations or explanations of dishes.

**Wine Pairing**: Consider wine pairing. A skilled sommelier can enhance your dining experience by suggesting wines that complement your meal.

**Pacing**: Savour each course. Fine dining is a leisurely experience; don't rush through your meal.

- **Elevating Your Taste Buds**

To truly elevate your taste buds during a gourmet dining experience, pay attention to these elements:

**Flavour Profiling:** Appreciate the nuances of flavours. Notice how different ingredients and seasonings interact on your palate.

**Texture**: Texture is as important as taste. Delight in the contrasts, from the crunch of a fresh salad to the tenderness of a perfectly cooked steak.

**Sensory Experience**: Engage all your senses. Observe the presentation, inhale the aromas, and listen to the sizzle of your dish.

**Saucery and Reductions**: Learn about sauces and reductions. They often play a pivotal role in fine dining, enhancing flavours and adding complexity.

**Tasting Menu**: Consider trying a tasting menu. These multi-course meals allow you to sample a variety of dishes, each crafted to perfection.

**Mindful Eating**: Be mindful of each bite. Focus on the food in front of you, and savour the experience without distractions.

- **The Role of Presentation**

Presentation is a fundamental aspect of gourmet dining:

**Plating**: Pay attention to how dishes are plated. Fine dining chefs are artists, and their creations are often visually stunning.

**Use of Colour**: Notice the use of colour. A well-arranged plate should have a balance of vibrant colours that are both appealing and appetising.

**Balance and Proportion**: The arrangement should have balance and proportion. Ingredients should be distributed harmoniously, creating a visual balance.

**Garnishes**: Garnishes are not just for show; they often provide additional flavours and textures that complement the main dish.

**Tableware**: Quality tableware is essential. Fine dining restaurants invest in elegant and unique plates, glasses, and utensils to enhance presentation.

**Edible Art**: In modern fine dining, some elements of the presentation may be edible, adding an element of surprise and delight.

By understanding and appreciating these aspects, you'll be well-prepared to embark on a memorable gourmet dining experience. Enjoy your culinary journey!

## Chapter 2: The Busy Professional's Kitchen

In the whirlwind of modern professional life, the kitchen often stands as an uncharted territory, an unexplored realm where time, skill, and convenience intersect.

For many, it becomes a place primarily associated with hurried breakfasts, takeout dinners, and the occasional late-night snack.

Yet, within these culinary confines lies an opportunity—an opportunity to transform the ordinary into the extraordinary, to craft gourmet experiences, and to savour the delight of finely crafted meals, all while navigating the demands of a bustling career.

Welcome to Chapter 2 of our culinary journey, where we venture into "**The Busy Professional's Kitchen**." Here, we will uncover the art of elevating your everyday cooking to gourmet heights without compromising on the demands of your busy life.

As we progress, we will delve into the essentials of equipping your culinary arsenal, optimising your kitchen for maximum efficiency, and introducing time-saving appliances that will become your trusted companions on this culinary expedition.

In this chapter, we invite you to rediscover your kitchen as a place of culinary wonder, where creativity and efficiency coexist.

Join us as we embark on a journey to transform your kitchen into a realm where gourmet dining is not a luxury, but a delightful everyday reality.

- **Equipping Your Culinary Arsenal**

To equip your culinary arsenal efficiently as a busy professional, consider the following:

**Essential Cookware**: Invest in high-quality pots, pans, and baking sheets. Look for non-stick options for easier cooking and cleaning.

**Knife Set**: A good set of knives is crucial. Make sure to include a chef's knife, paring knife, and serrated knife. Keep them sharp for precise cutting.

**Utensils**: Stock your kitchen with essential utensils like spatulas, tongs, wooden spoons, and a whisk. These tools will make cooking and stirring easier.

**Mixing Bowls**: Various sizes of mixing bowls are versatile for preparing ingredients and mixing recipes.

**Measuring Tools**: Accurate measuring cups and spoons are essential for following recipes precisely.

**Cutting Boards**: Have separate cutting boards for meats and vegetables to avoid cross-contamination.

**Storage Containers**: Invest in a variety of airtight containers to store leftovers and ingredients.

- **Organising Your Kitchen for Efficiency**

Efficient kitchen organisation is key for a busy professional:

**Declutter**: Remove items you rarely use. Keep only what you need to avoid clutter.

**Zone Your Kitchen**: Group similar items together. For example, create a baking zone, a cooking zone, and a prep zone.

**Label Shelves and Drawers**: Use labels to identify where everything belongs. It saves time searching for items.

**Fridge and Pantry**: Regularly check and organise your fridge and pantry. Rotate items to use older ingredients first.

**Spice Organization**: Use a spice rack or drawer inserts to keep spices accessible and organised.

**Vertical Storage**: Use hooks, racks, and shelves on walls and inside cabinet doors to maximise space.

- **Time-Saving Appliances**

Time-saving appliances can be a game-changer:

**Slow Cooker:** Ideal for preparing meals while you work. Throw in ingredients in the morning, and dinner is ready when you get home.

**Instant Pot:** Combines several cooking methods in one appliance, making it perfect for quick meals.

**Food Processor:** Speeds up chopping, slicing, and shredding tasks significantly.

**Blender:** Great for smoothies, soups, and sauces. Invest in a high-quality blender for smooth results.

**Microwave:** Don't underestimate its convenience for reheating and quick cooking.

**Toaster Oven:** Faster than a regular oven for small meals or reheating.

**Coffee Maker with a Timer:** Wake up to freshly brewed coffee or tea

## Chapter 3: Mastering the Basics

Welcome to Chapter 3 of your culinary journey, where we'll dive deep into the foundational skills that every home chef should possess.

In this chapter, you will acquire the knowledge and techniques that form the bedrock of exceptional cooking.

From wielding a knife with precision to mastering essential cooking techniques and understanding the science of flavours, we will equip you with the skills necessary to elevate your culinary creations.

In this chapter, we'll begin by honing your **Knife Skills**, ensuring you can chop, slice, and dice like a professional.

Then, we'll explore **Essential Cooking Techniques**, providing you with the confidence to sear, sauté, and simmer your way to culinary excellence.

Finally, we'll uncover the fascinating world of **The Science of Flavors**, delving into the secrets behind creating perfectly balanced and delectable dishes

- **Knife Skills: Chop Like a Pro**

Mastering knife skills is crucial in the world of cooking.

**Choosing the Right Knife**: Start by selecting the appropriate knife for the task at hand. A chef's knife is versatile for most tasks, while a paring knife is perfect for precision.

**Proper Grip**: Hold the knife with a firm but not overly tight grip. Your index finger and thumb should be on either side of the blade's base, with your other fingers wrapping around the handle.

**Knife Maintenance**: Keep your knife sharp through regular honing and sharpening. A sharp knife is safer and more efficient.

**Cutting Techniques**: Learn various cutting techniques like the julienne, chiffonade, and brunoise. Practise each to become proficient.

**Guiding Hand**: Use your non-dominant hand to hold and guide the food. Curl your fingertips inward to avoid accidents.

**Basic Cuts**: Practise basic cuts such as slicing, dicing, and chopping. Pay attention to consistent thickness for even cooking.

**Speed and Precision**: As you progress, work on improving your speed while maintaining precision. This comes with practice and confidence.

- **Essential Cooking Techniques**

Cooking techniques are the building blocks of great dishes.

**Searing:** Master the art of searing meats and vegetables to create a flavorful crust. Preheat your pan, add oil, and ensure the food is dry for the best results.

**Sautéing:** Learn the technique of sautéing, which involves cooking food quickly in a small amount of oil over high heat. Stir constantly for even cooking.

**Simmering and Boiling**: Understand the differences between simmering and boiling. Simmering is gentle bubbling, while boiling is vigorous. Use each as appropriate for your recipes.

**Braising**: Explore the slow-cooking method of braising to tenderise tougher cuts of meat. This involves searing, then simmering with liquid in a covered pot.

**Roasting**: Perfect your roasting skills for meats and vegetables. Use a roasting pan, rack, and proper seasoning for delicious results.

**Grilling**: Experiment with grilling for a smoky flavour. Control the heat and use direct and indirect grilling methods for various foods.

**Baking**: Delve into baking for bread, pastries, and desserts. Understand the importance of precise measurements and temperature control

- **The Science of Flavours**

Creating flavorful dishes involves understanding the science behind taste and aroma.

**Taste Components**: Learn about the five basic tastes - sweet, salty, sour, bitter, and umami. Understand how they interact in recipes.

**Aromas and Odours**: Discover the role of aromas and how they impact our perception of flavour. Ingredients like herbs, spices, and aromatics play a crucial role.

**Balancing Flavours**: Master the art of balancing flavours. Sweetness can counter bitterness, acidity can brighten a dish, and umami can add depth.

**Seasoning Techniques**: Experiment with different ways to season dishes, such as layering flavours, marinating, and using finishing touches like fresh herbs.

**Chemical Reactions**: Explore the chemical reactions that occur during cooking, like caramelization and Maillard browning, which enhance flavour.

**Experimentation**: Don't be afraid to experiment with new ingredients and flavour combinations. Keep a palate journal to document your discoveries.

## Chapter 4: The Gourmet Pantry

Welcome to the heart of gourmet cooking—**the pantry**. Just as an artist relies on a palette of colours to create a masterpiece, a gourmet chef depends on a well-stocked pantry to craft culinary delights.

In this chapter, we will delve into the art of stocking your pantry with essential ingredients that form the foundation of gourmet cuisine.

A gourmet pantry is a treasure trove of flavours, textures, and possibilities. It is where creativity and convenience intersect, allowing you to transform ordinary ingredients into extraordinary dishes.

From the staples that provide sustenance to the spices that awaken the senses, and the oils and vinegars that elevate flavours, we'll explore each facet in-depth.

Whether you're an aspiring home chef or a seasoned epicurean, this chapter will guide you through the process of building and maintaining a gourmet pantry that will inspire your culinary adventures.

So, let's embark on this gastronomic journey, starting with the art of stocking up on pantry staples, followed by the secrets of spicing up your life, and finally, unlocking the potential of gourmet oils and vinegars. Prepare to elevate your cooking to gourmet heights.

- **Stocking Up on Staples**

**Grains and Legumes**: A well-stocked pantry includes various grains like rice (jasmine, basmati, arborio), pasta, quinoa, and lentils. These form the foundation for many dishes.

**Canned Goods**: Keep canned tomatoes, beans, and vegetables for convenience. They're handy for soups, stews, and quick meals.

**Flour and Baking Supplies**: All-purpose flour, whole wheat flour, and baking powder are key for baking. Don't forget sugar, salt, and yeast.

**Herbs and Spices**: Stock dried herbs like oregano, thyme, and bay leaves. For spices, include basics like cinnamon, paprika, cumin, and chili powder.

**Nuts and Seeds**: Almonds, walnuts, and pine nuts add texture and flavour to dishes. Also, consider sesame seeds, sunflower seeds, and flaxseeds.

**Pantry Proteins**: Tinned tuna, salmon, or chicken can be used in salads and sandwiches.

**Pasta and Sauces**: High-quality pasta and a variety of pasta sauces (tomato, Alfredo, pesto) enhance your culinary options.

- **Spice Up Your Life: The Spice Rack Essentials**

**Salt and Pepper:** Invest in high-quality sea salt and freshly ground black pepper. These are fundamental in seasoning.

**Herbs**: Dried herbs like basil, oregano, rosemary, and thyme are versatile for Italian, Mediterranean, or French cuisine.

**Spices**: Essentials include ground cumin, coriander, paprika, and cinnamon. Experiment with whole spices like cloves, cardamom, and mustard seeds for Indian and Asian dishes.

**Chilli**: Have various types of chilli on hand, such as chilli flakes, cayenne, and chilli powder for heat and flavour.

**Curry Powders and Garam Masala**: These are essential for Indian and South Asian cooking.

**Vanilla Extract**: For baking and desserts, use pure vanilla extract.

**Citrus Zest**: Lemon and orange zest add brightness to dishes.

- **Gourmet Oils and Vinegars**

**Olive Oil**: Extra virgin olive oil is a kitchen staple. Use it for sautéing, dressings, and finishing dishes. Consider a robust one for bold flavours and a mild one for delicate dishes.

**Vegetable Oil:** A neutral oil like canola or grapeseed is suitable for high-heat cooking and baking.

**Nut Oils**: Walnut, almond, and hazelnut oils impart unique flavours to salads and desserts.

**Sesame Oil**: Essential in Asian cuisine, both toasted and regular sesame oil can be used for different purposes.

**Vinegars**: Keep a variety of vinegars like balsamic, red wine, white wine, and rice vinegar. They're crucial for dressings and marinades.

**Infused Oils and Vinegars:** Experiment with flavoured oils and vinegars for a gourmet touch. Examples include truffle oil and raspberry vinegar.

Remember to store these pantry items properly, in a cool, dark place to maintain their quality. Regularly check expiration dates to ensure freshness. Building a well-stocked pantry enhances your cooking versatility.

## Chapter 5: From Quick Bites to Culinary Feats

In this culinary journey, we embark on a quest to master the art of time-efficient yet delectable cooking.

Whether you're seeking to kickstart your day with a quick and satisfying breakfast, conquer the challenges of office lunches, or leave a lasting impression on dinner guests without breaking a sweat, this chapter 5 is your culinary compass.

From dawn to dusk, we'll explore the realms of culinary creativity, showing you how to turn the mundane into the extraordinary.

Whether you have just minutes to spare or are looking to hone your skills for special occasions, our in-depth guidance will equip you with the knowledge and techniques needed to elevate your culinary prowess.

Prepare to uncover the secrets of **Quick and Delectable Breakfasts** that jumpstart your day, discover the **Office Lunch Hacks** that make your workdays more enjoyable, and master the art of **Impressing Dinner Guests in Minutes**.

Let's dive into the world of flavours, convenience, and culinary delights that will leave you inspired and your taste buds craving for more.

- **Quick and Delectable Breakfasts**

**Overnight Oats**: Prepare a batch the night before by mixing oats, milk or yogurt, and your favourite toppings like berries, nuts, or honey. In the morning, you'll have a nutritious breakfast ready to eat.

**Smoothie Bowls**: Blend fruits, yogurt, and a handful of greens like spinach or kale for a refreshing breakfast. Top it with granola, seeds, and more fruits for texture and flavour.

**Eggs in Various Ways**: Try scrambled eggs, poached eggs, or omelettes. Add veggies, cheese, and herbs for extra flavour. Serve with whole-grain toast or avocado

**Avocado Toast**: Mash ripe avocado on whole-grain toast. Add toppings like sliced tomatoes, a poached egg, or smoked salmon. Drizzle with olive oil and sprinkle with salt and pepper.

- **Office Lunch Hacks**

**Prep Ahead:** Spend some time on Sunday prepping ingredients like grilled chicken, roasted veggies, and quinoa. Use them throughout the week to assemble quick salads or grain bowls.

**Mason Jar Salads**: Layer salad ingredients in a mason jar with dressing at the bottom. Shake it up when it's time to eat for a fresh and crisp salad.

**Leftovers Makeovers**: Transform dinner leftovers into exciting lunches. For example, turn last night's stir-fry into a wrap or use roasted vegetables in a pasta salad.

**Batch Cook and Freeze**: Prepare large batches of soups, stews, or casseroles on the weekends and freeze individual portions. Reheat them in the office microwave for a hearty lunch.

- **Impressing Dinner Guests in Minutes**

**Simple Appetisers**: Offer elegant yet quick appetisers like bruschetta, a cheese platter, or stuffed mushrooms. These set the tone for a great meal.

**One-Pan Dinners**: Opt for dishes that cook in one pan, like chicken piccata or shrimp scampi. They're flavorful and reduce cleanup.

**Fresh Ingredients**: Use high-quality, fresh ingredients. A simple salad with ripe tomatoes and mozzarella drizzled with balsamic glaze can be impressive.

**Dessert Shortcut**: Prepare a semi-homemade dessert like chocolate-dipped strawberries or a store-bought tart with whipped cream.

Remember to focus on presentation, ambiance, and being a gracious host to create a memorable dining experience.

## Chapter 6: The Art of Menu Planning

Welcome to Chapter 6 of "**The Art of Menu Planning**."

In this chapter, we embark on a culinary journey where meal planning becomes an art form, and your kitchen transforms into a canvas for creativity and nourishment.

Crafting a well-balanced menu is not merely about satisfying hunger; it's about orchestrating a harmonious symphony of flavours, textures, and nutrition that caters to your palate and lifestyle.

As we delve deeper into the intricacies of menu planning, we will explore three vital aspects, each essential to master the culinary canvas:

**Crafting a Weekly Culinary Calendar** - Here, you'll learn how to paint your week with an array of dishes that match your schedule and preferences. We'll guide you through the process of selecting ingredients, planning for variety, and ensuring that your meals align seamlessly with your weekly routines.

**Balancing Nutritional Needs** - Nutrition is the palette that colours our health and vitality. In this section, we'll provide you with the brushes and paints needed to create meals that not only tantalise your taste buds but also fuel your body optimally. From understanding macros to portion control, you'll gain the expertise to design menus that prioritise well-being.

**Incorporating Global Flavours** - The world is a vast treasure trove of culinary delights. We'll take you on a journey around the globe, exploring the vibrant tapestry of international cuisines. You'll discover how to infuse your menus with the rich, diverse flavours of various cultures, adding an exciting and adventurous dimension to your dining experiences.

So, whether you're a seasoned home chef or just starting your culinary voyage, prepare to elevate your menu planning skills to an art form.

Let's begin our exploration, unlocking the secrets to crafting a weekly culinary calendar, balancing nutritional needs, and incorporating global flavours that will turn your meals into masterpieces.

- **Crafting a Weekly Culinary Calendar**

Start by assessing your weekly schedule. Consider days when you have more or less time for cooking, as this will influence your menu choices.

Take stock of your pantry and ingredients on hand before planning. This helps reduce waste and saves money.

Plan for variety by including different protein sources (meat, fish, beans, tofu), grains (rice, pasta, quinoa), and vegetables.

Incorporate theme nights (e.g., Taco Tuesday or Meatless Monday) to add excitement to your menu.

Create a shopping list based on your planned meals to ensure you have all the necessary ingredients.

Be flexible and open to changes in case unexpected events arise during the week.

- **Balancing Nutritional Needs**

Understand the basics of macronutrients: carbohydrates, proteins, and fats, and how they contribute to your diet.

Calculate your daily caloric needs based on your goals (maintenance, weight loss, or gain) and activity level..

Use tools like food diaries or apps to track your intake and assess if you're meeting your nutritional goals.

Pay attention to portion sizes to avoid overeating, and consider using smaller plates to help with portion control.

Learn about micronutrients (vitamins and minerals) and their importance in maintaining overall health.

If you have specific dietary needs or restrictions, consult with a registered dietitian for personalised guidance.

- **Incorporating Global Flavors**

Explore the culinary traditions of different regions, such as Asian, Mediterranean, Latin American, and Middle Eastern cuisines.

Study the key ingredients, herbs, and spices that define these cuisines and learn how to use them in your cooking.

Experiment with cooking techniques unique to each cuisine, like stir-frying, grilling, or slow braising.

Start with simple recipes and gradually build your skills in preparing international dishes. Visit ethnic grocery stores

## Chapter 7: Savory Secrets for Busy Professionals

In the whirlwind of a busy professional life, finding the time to prepare delicious and nutritious meals can often feel like an insurmountable challenge.

But fear not, for within these pages, we have unlocked the **Savory Secrets** that will revolutionise your approach to cooking, making gourmet meals a quick and achievable reality even on the most hectic of days.

Our culinary journey begins with an exploration of three culinary domains - **Speedy Soups and Stews, One-Pan Wonders, and Stir-Fry Simplified**.

In this chapter 7, we will delve deep into these cooking techniques, providing you with the skills and insights to master each one.

With our expert guidance, you'll not only save precious time but also savour the satisfaction of crafting mouthwatering dishes that leave a lasting impression.

Join us as we uncover the art of whipping up hearty soups and stews in record time, transforming a single pan into a canvas for culinary creations that require minimal cleanup, and demystifying the fast-paced world of stir-frying.

Whether you're a seasoned chef or a novice in the kitchen, these savoury secrets will equip you to create gourmet meals with ease, ensuring that your busy professional life is enriched with the pleasures of fine dining, right in the comfort of your own home.

Let's embark on this culinary adventure together!

- **Speedy Soups and Stews**

**Start with a good base**: Use pre-made broth or stock to save time. You can also prepare a large batch of homemade broth in advance and freeze it in portions.

**Chop ingredients in advance**: Prepping your vegetables and proteins ahead of time can significantly speed up the cooking process.

**Utilise a pressure cooker**: Pressure cookers can drastically reduce cooking times for soups and stews. They are especially handy for tough cuts of meat.

**Consider canned or frozen ingredients**: Items like canned beans or frozen vegetables are convenient and can be added directly to your soups and stews.

**Simmer for flavour**: While speed is essential, allowing your soups and stews to simmer for a bit can enhance the depth of flavour. Just let it simmer while you attend to other tasks.

- **One-Pan Wonders**

**Choose the right pan**: A versatile, high-quality pan is essential for one-pan dishes. Look for non-stick or cast iron options.

**Prep ingredients uniformly**: Cut ingredients to similar sizes to ensure even cooking.

**Layer flavours** : Start by browning meats or aromatics to build a flavorful base, then add vegetables and starches.

**Control heat:** Pay attention to heat levels to prevent burning or overcooking. Use medium-high heat for searing and browning, and reduce to simmer for gentle cooking.

**Don't overcrowd the pan**: Overcrowding can lead to uneven cooking. Cook in batches if necessary or use a larger pan

- **Stir-Fry Simplified**

**Gather your mise en place**: Have all your ingredients chopped, sauces mixed, and seasonings ready before starting.

Stir-frying is a quick process.

**High heat is key**: Stir-frying is all about high heat and quick cooking. Use a wok or a wide skillet to ensure even heating.

**Cook in stages**: Add ingredients to the pan in stages, starting with items that require the most cooking time. This prevents overcooking or undercooking.

**Keep it moving**: Continuously stir or toss the ingredients to avoid sticking and ensure even cooking.

**Sauce at the end**: Add your stir-fry sauce toward the end of cooking to prevent sogginess and ensure a flavorful finish.

Remember that practice makes perfect, and don't be afraid to experiment with flavours and ingredients to suit your preferences and dietary needs. Enjoy your culinary adventures!

## Chapter 8: Effortless Elegance

In the realm of culinary mastery, there exists a delightful paradox—a realm where elegance meets simplicity.

Chapter 8 beckons you into this world of gastronomic finesse, where the art of crafting unforgettable dishes is demystified.

Here, we embark on a journey where culinary sophistication seamlessly intertwines with ease, where every bite is a testament to the power of simplicity in the pursuit of exceptional taste.

As we venture further, we will unlock the secrets behind creating show-stopping salads that burst with flavour and colour unveiling the art of crafting simple yet stunning appetisers that leave a lasting impression on your guests, and demystifying the creation of decadent desserts that will have your loved ones swooning.

Join us in the exploration of **Effortless Elegance,** where we transform ordinary ingredients into extraordinary delights, proving that the path to culinary mastery is not always laden with complexity but can often be paved with grace and simplicity.

Let's dive deep into the heart of these culinary endeavours, where taste and presentation converge to create moments of pure gastronomic delight.

- **Creating Show-Stopping Salads**

**Choosing Your Greens**: Start with a base of fresh greens. Options like spinach, arugula, romaine, or mixed greens work well.

**Texture Variety**: Add a variety of textures for interest. Consider ingredients like toasted nuts, crispy bacon, or croutons.

**Colourful Veggies**: Incorporate colourful vegetables such as cherry tomatoes, bell peppers, and red onions for a vibrant look.

**Protein**: Enhance your salad with protein sources like grilled chicken, shrimp, or tofu.

**Cheese**: Don't forget a sprinkle of cheese – options like feta, goat cheese, or Parmesan can elevate the flavour.

**Dressing**: Create a homemade dressing with a balanced ratio of oil, vinegar, and seasonings. Experiment with flavours like balsamic vinaigrette or honey mustard.

**Toppings**: Finish with a handful of toppings like dried cranberries, avocado slices, or pomegranate seeds for an extra pop of flavour

- **Simple Yet Stunning Appetisers**

**Bruschetta**: Toast slices of baguette, rub with garlic, and top with diced tomatoes, fresh basil, and a drizzle of balsamic glaze.

**Stuffed Mushrooms**: Hollow out mushroom caps and stuff with a mixture of cream cheese, garlic, herbs, and breadcrumbs. Bake until golden.

**Caprese Skewers**: Thread cherry tomatoes, fresh mozzarella, and basil leaves onto skewers. Drizzle with olive oil and balsamic reduction.

**Spinach and Artichoke Dip**: Combine spinach, artichoke hearts, cream cheese, and Parmesan. Bake until bubbly and serve with tortilla chips.

**Deviled Eggs**: Make classic deviled eggs with a twist by adding ingredients like smoked paprika, Sriracha, or bacon bits.

- **Decadent Desserts Made Easy**

**Chocolate Fondue**: Melt chocolate with heavy cream and dip fruits, marshmallows, or pretzels for a fun dessert experience.

**Tiramisu**: Layer coffee-soaked ladyfingers with a mascarpone cheese mixture, then dust with cocoa powder.

**No-Bake Cheesecake**: Whip up a simple cheesecake filling, pour it into a graham cracker crust, and refrigerate until set. Top with fresh fruit or a fruit compote.

**Molten Lava Cakes**: Bake individual chocolate cakes with a gooey centre. Serve warm with a scoop of vanilla ice cream.

**Fruit Tart**: Create a pastry crust, fill it with pastry cream, and top with fresh sliced fruits like berries, kiwi, and peaches. Brush with apricot glaze for shine.

Remember, the key to effortless elegance in your dishes is the presentation. Use nice plating techniques, garnishes, and serving dishes to make your salads, appetisers, and desserts visually appealing.

Enjoy creating these delightful dishes!

## **Chapter 9: Dining Out Like a Pro**

Dining out isn't just about satisfying hunger; it's an opportunity to savour new flavours, explore culinary traditions, and create memorable experiences.

Whether you're a seasoned food enthusiast or a casual diner, this chapter will equip you with the knowledge and confidence to navigate the world of restaurants like a pro.

In the following sections, we'll delve into three crucial aspects of dining out: "**Navigating Restaurant Menus with Confidence,**" "**Wine Pairing Wisdom,**" and "**Tipping Etiquette for Discerning Diners.**"

Each of these areas plays a pivotal role in enhancing your dining experience and ensuring that you leave the restaurant not only satisfied but with a sense of culinary fulfilment.

So, let's embark on this gastronomic journey together, arming you with the skills to select dishes with finesse, elevate your meal with the perfect wine pairing, and navigate the sometimes intricate world of tipping etiquette.

By the end of this chapter, you'll be dining out with the poise and expertise of a true connoisseur, ready to savour every bite and sip, no matter where your culinary adventures take you.

- Navigating Restaurant Menus with Confidence

When it comes to navigating restaurant menus with confidence, consider these tips:

**Study the Menu in Advance**: Many restaurants post their menus online. Take a look before you go to get an idea of the dishes they offer.

**Ask for Recommendations**: Don't hesitate to ask your server for suggestions. They often know the menu inside out and can guide you based on your preferences.

**Consider Dietary Restrictions**: If you have dietary restrictions or allergies, inform your server. They can help you find suitable options or make accommodations.

**Balance Your Meal**: Aim for a balanced meal with a variety of flavours, textures, and courses. Start with an appetiser, choose a main course, and maybe indulge in dessert.

**Explore Local Specialties**: When dining in a new place, try local specialties. It's a great way to experience the culture through food.

- **Wine Pairing Wisdom**

Pairing wine with your meal can enhance the dining experience.

Here's how to do it wisely:

**Match Intensity**: Consider the intensity of your dish. Lighter dishes like seafood go well with white wines, while heavier meats pair nicely with reds.

**Complement Flavours:** Choose wines that complement the flavours in your food. For example, a spicy dish can be balanced with a slightly sweet wine.

**Consider Acidity**: High-acid wines like Sauvignon Blanc can cut through rich, fatty dishes, while low-acid wines like Chardonnay work well with creamy sauces.

**Experiment**: Don't be afraid to try new pairings. Experimenting with wine and food combinations can lead to delightful discoveries.

**Ask for Guidance**: If you're unsure, ask the sommelier or your server for wine recommendations. They can suggest options that will enhance your meal.

- **Tipping Etiquette for Discerning Diners**

Tipping etiquette can vary by region, but here are some general guidelines:

**Check the Bill**: Most restaurants include a suggested tip on the bill. You can follow this, but it's not mandatory.

**Consider Service Quality**: Your tip should reflect the quality of service you received. If the service was exceptional, consider tipping more generously.

**Know Local Customs**: In some countries, tipping is not common or is included in the service charge. Research the local customs when travelling.

**Splitting the Bill**: If you're dining with a group, check if the gratuity is already included. If not, discuss how you'll split the tip fairly.

**Cash or Card**: You can tip in cash or add it to your card payment. Both methods are generally acceptable.

**Express Appreciation:** A simple "thank you" along with your tip is a nice way to show appreciation for good service.

Remember that tipping practices can vary, so it's essential to be aware of the customs wherever you dine to ensure you're following local etiquette.

# Chapter 10: Hosting Impromptu Gatherings

In the world of hosting, spontaneity can lead to some of the most memorable moments.

Whether it's a last-minute dinner party, an impromptu cocktail hour, or a buffet spread put together on the fly, the ability to welcome friends and family with open arms, even at a moment's notice, is a skill worth mastering.

In this chapter, we delve into the art of **hosting impromptu gatherings** with finesse and flair.

We'll guide you through the intricacies of last-minute dinner parties, help you master the art of hosting a bustling cocktail hour even when you're short on time, and provide you with the secrets to buffet brilliance that will leave your guests raving about your hospitality.

So, embrace the unexpected and join us as we explore the world of spontaneous entertaining.

With a dash of creativity, a sprinkle of preparedness, and a generous helping of hospitality, you'll be ready to host unforgettable impromptu gatherings that bring joy and warmth to any occasion.

Let's get started!

- **Last-Minute Dinner Parties**

**Keep a Well-Stocked Pantry**: Always have some versatile ingredients on hand, such as pasta, canned tomatoes, olive oil, and spices. These can be used to whip up a variety of last-minute dishes.

**Simple Yet Impressive Menu**: Opt for dishes that are easy to prepare but still taste gourmet. For example, pasta with homemade pesto or a seared chicken breast with a flavorful sauce.

**Delegate and Collaborate**: If guests offer to bring something, don't hesitate to accept. It eases your workload and makes guests feel involved. Assign specific dishes or drinks to bring to avoid overlap.

**Set the Mood**: Even a last-minute dinner can feel special with the right atmosphere. Dim the lights, light some candles, and put on some background music to create a cozy ambiance.

**Quick Cleanup Plan**: Use disposable plates and utensils to minimise cleanup. Keep a trash bag handy, and as the party winds down, encourage guests to help tidy up.

- **Cocktail Hour for the Busy Host**

**Signature Cocktails**: Create one or two signature cocktails that are easy to prepare and serve. Pre-mix them in large batches if possible.

**Snack Selection**: Offer a variety of simple yet delicious snacks like nuts, olives, cheese, and charcuterie. These can be prepared in advance and require minimal effort.

**Chill Drinks in Advance**: Ensure that your drinks, both alcoholic and non-alcoholic, are properly chilled before the guests arrive. Use ice buckets or a cooler to keep them cold throughout the event.

**Efficient Bar Setup**: Set up a self-serve drink station with all the necessary ingredients, garnishes, and glassware. This allows guests to help themselves, reducing the need for constant bartending.

**Keep It Casual**: Cocktail hour is often more relaxed than a full dinner party, so encourage mingling and conversation. Create comfortable seating areas and encourage guests to move around.

- **Buffet Brilliance**

**Balanced Menu**: Plan a menu with a variety of dishes that cater to different tastes and dietary preferences. Include options for vegetarians, vegans, and those with food allergies.

**Presentation Matters**: Use attractive serving platters and garnishes to make your buffet visually appealing. Consider using tiered stands to add height to the display.

**Label Everything**: Clearly label each dish, especially if it contains allergens or unusual ingredients. This helps guests make informed choices.

**Keep It Hot or Cold**: Use chafing dishes or ice trays to maintain the temperature of hot and cold dishes. Food safety is crucial for a buffet.

**Flow and Space**: Arrange the buffet table so that there's a logical flow for guests to follow. Make sure there's enough space for people to move comfortably and access the food.

Remember, the key to successful impromptu gatherings is to stay calm, be adaptable, and focus on creating a welcoming and enjoyable atmosphere for your guests.

## Chapter 11: Travelling the World through Your Plate

The world is a vast and diverse tapestry of cultures, each with its unique customs, traditions, and, perhaps most enticingly, its own culinary treasures.

While jet-setting across the globe might not always be feasible, there exists a remarkable passport that grants you access to these far-flung destinations without ever leaving your kitchen – the rich and flavorful world of international cuisine.

In this chapter, we invite you on a journey that transcends borders, connecting you with the globe's myriad tastes and traditions. It's a journey that can be embarked upon at your own pace, accommodating even the busiest of schedules.

So fasten your apron, sharpen your culinary curiosity, and prepare to embark on an adventure where the only passport you need is a plate.

We'll begin by delving into the concept of **"Global Cuisine at Your Fingertips,"** where we'll provide you with in-depth guidance on how to explore the world's flavours without crossing time zones.

Then, for the ever-busy traveller yearning to bring a piece of their journeys home, we'll offer insights into selecting and preserving **"Culinary Souvenirs."**

Finally, we'll unveil a treasure trove of "**Authentic Recipes from Around the Globe**," offering detailed instructions to recreate dishes that transport your senses to far-off lands.

Whether you're an aspiring chef, a seasoned home cook, or simply someone with a taste for adventure, these pages hold the keys to unlocking the world through your plate.

So, let's begin this culinary expedition, where each meal is a ticket to a new destination, and each bite is a glimpse into the heart and soul of a different culture.

Bon appétit, or as they say in other corners of the world, ¡buen provecho, bon appétit, and smaklig måltid! (Enjoy your meal!)

- **Global Cuisine at Your Fingertips**

In this section, you can explore the diverse world of global cuisine without leaving your kitchen.

Start by researching the cuisines of different countries or regions you're interested in.

Learn about their staple ingredients, cooking techniques, and flavour profiles. Invest in essential spices and condiments from these regions to keep in your pantry.

To truly immerse yourself, try the following:

**Cooking Classes**: Sign up for online cooking classes or workshops specialising in various international cuisines. Many platforms offer live sessions where you can interact with experienced chefs.

**Cookbooks**: Invest in cookbooks dedicated to global cuisines. These often provide detailed recipes, cultural context, and cooking tips.

**Local Ingredients**: Whenever possible, source authentic ingredients from specialty stores or online retailers. For example, if you're exploring Thai cuisine, look for Thai basil, lemongrass, and fish sauce.

**Practice**: Don't be afraid to experiment and practice. Start with simpler recipes and gradually tackle more complex dishes.

- **Culinary Souvenirs for the Busy Traveller**

For those with busy schedules, bringing back culinary souvenirs from your travels can be a wonderful way to savour the memories.

Here's how to do it effectively:

**Research Local Products**: Before your trip, research and make a list of unique local food products from your destination. This could include spices, sauces, chocolates, or specialty snacks.

**Packaging**: Ensure your chosen culinary souvenirs are well-packaged and won't spoil during travel. Use airtight containers or jars for liquids.

**Check Regulations:** Be aware of customs regulations regarding food items when travelling internationally. Some items may not be allowed into certain countries.

**Storage**: Once back home, store your culinary souvenirs properly. Keep them in a cool, dark place to maintain freshness.

**Savour and Share**: Enjoy these treats with friends and family, and share stories about your travels through the flavours you've brought home.

- **Authentic Recipes from Around the Globe**

Cooking authentic recipes from different parts of the world can be a rewarding experience.

Here's how to go about it:

**Research Recipes:** Start by finding reputable sources for authentic recipes. Look for cookbooks, online food blogs, or websites run by chefs from the respective regions.

**Ingredients**: Gather all the necessary ingredients, including any that might be hard to find locally. Specialty ethnic grocery stores or online retailers can be helpful.

**Techniques**: Pay close attention to cooking techniques and methods. Authenticity often lies in the way dishes are prepared.

**Presentation**: Presentation is key to authentic cuisine. Learn about traditional plating styles and garnishes used in that specific cuisine.

**Taste Test**: Invite friends or family to try the dishes with you. Encourage them to provide feedback, and refine

# Recipes

The following recipes offer a range of complexity, from quick and easy options for busy professionals to more intricate and elegant choices for special occasions or adventurous cooks. They represent some of the most beloved gourmet dishes from various culinary traditions.

**Quick Gourmet Recipes:*

These quick gourmet recipes are perfect for a delicious meal, without a lot of time in the kitchen. Enjoy

### Grilled Lemon-Herb Chicken Breast

A flavorful and healthy chicken dish that's ready in under 30 minutes.

Ingredients:
- 4 boneless, skinless chicken breasts
- 2 tablespoons olive oil
- Zest and juice of 1 lemon
- 2 cloves garlic, minced
- 1 tablespoon fresh herbs (such as rosemary, thyme, or basil), chopped
- Salt and pepper to taste

Preparation:
1. In a bowl, combine olive oil, lemon zest, lemon juice, minced garlic, fresh herbs, salt, and pepper to create a marinade.
2. Place chicken breasts in a zip-top bag or a shallow dish and pour the marinade over them.
3. Seal the bag or cover the dish and refrigerate for 15-20 minutes.
4. Preheat your grill or grill pan to medium-high heat.
5. Grill chicken for about 6-8 minutes per side or until it reaches an internal temperature of 165°F (74°C).

Estimated Total Time: Approximately 30 minutes

### Pasta Aglio e Olio

An Italian classic with simple yet exquisite flavours, ready in 20 minutes.

Ingredients:
- 8 ounces spaghetti or linguine
- 1/4 cup extra-virgin olive oil
- 4 cloves garlic, thinly sliced
- 1/2 teaspoon red pepper flakes (adjust to taste)
- Fresh parsley, chopped
- Grated Parmesan cheese
- Salt and pepper to taste

Preparation:
1. Cook pasta according to package instructions until al dente. Drain and set aside.
2. In a large skillet, heat olive oil over low heat. Add sliced garlic and red pepper flakes. Cook until garlic turns golden (about 2-3 minutes), being careful not to burn it.
3. Add cooked pasta to the skillet, tossing to coat with the garlic-infused oil.
4. Season with salt, pepper, and fresh parsley.
5. Serve with grated Parmesan cheese on top.

Estimated Total Time: Approximately 20 minutes

## Shrimp Scampi

Succulent shrimp cooked in a garlic and butter sauce, served over linguine, taking around 25 minutes to prepare.

Ingredients:

- 1 pound large shrimp, peeled and deveined
- 8 ounces linguine or spaghetti
- 3 tablespoons unsalted butter
- 3 tablespoons olive oil
- 4 cloves garlic, minced
- 1/4 cup white wine (optional)
- Juice of 1 lemon
- Fresh parsley, chopped
- Red pepper flakes (optional)
- Salt and pepper to taste

Preparation:
1. Cook pasta according to package instructions until al dente. Drain and set aside.
2. In a large skillet, heat butter and olive oil over medium-high heat.
3. Add minced garlic and sauté for about 1 minute until fragrant.
4. Add shrimp and cook for 2-3 minutes per side until they turn pink.
5. If using, pour in white wine and lemon juice, allowing it to simmer for 2-3 minutes.
6. Season with salt, pepper, chopped parsley, and red pepper flakes (if desired).
7. Serve the shrimp and sauce over cooked linguine.

Estimated Total Time: Approximately 25 minutes

**Intermediate Gourmet Recipes:*

These intermediate gourmet recipes offer rich and complex flavours, making them perfect for special occasions or when you want to impress your guests with a delicious meal.

# Coq au Vin

A French classic featuring slow-cooked chicken in red wine with mushrooms and onions.

Ingredients:

- 4 chicken leg quarters (thighs and drumsticks)
- 4 slices of bacon, chopped
- 1 onion, chopped
- 2 cloves garlic, minced
- 1 carrot, chopped
- 1 celery stalk, chopped
- 1 bottle (750ml) red wine (such as Burgundy)
- 2 cups chicken broth
- 2 tablespoons tomato paste
- 10-12 small pearl onions, peeled
- 8 ounces mushrooms, quartered
- 2 tablespoons all-purpose flour
- 2 tablespoons butter
- Fresh thyme sprigs
- Salt and pepper to taste

Preparation:

1. In a large Dutch oven, cook the chopped bacon until crispy. Remove bacon and set aside.
2. Season chicken with salt and pepper, then brown them in the bacon fat. Remove and set aside.
3. In the same pot, sauté onions, garlic, carrot, and celery until softened.
4. Add tomato paste and cook for a few minutes.
5. Return chicken and bacon to the pot. Pour in red wine and chicken broth. Add thyme sprigs.
6. Cover and simmer for about 1 hour until the chicken is tender.
7. In a separate pan, melt butter and sauté pearl onions and mushrooms until browned.
8. Sprinkle flour over the mushroom mixture, stirring to create a roux.
9. Add the mushroom mixture to the chicken, cooking for an additional 15-20 minutes.
10. Adjust seasoning and serve hot.

Estimated Total Time: Approximately 2 hours

## Beef Bourguignon

Another French favourite, this slow-cooked beef stew is rich and savoury, perfect for special occasions.

Ingredients:

2 pounds beef stew meat (such as chuck)
4 slices of bacon, chopped
1 onion, chopped
2 cloves garlic, minced
2 carrots, chopped
2 celery stalks, chopped
1 bottle (750ml) red wine (such as Burgundy)
2 cups beef broth
2 tablespoons tomato paste
1 bouquet garni (thyme, bay leaves, parsley)
8 ounces pearl onions, peeled
8 ounces mushrooms, quartered
2 tablespoons all-purpose flour
2 tablespoons butter
Salt and pepper to taste

Preparation:

1. In a large Dutch oven, cook the chopped bacon until crispy. Remove bacon and set aside.
2. Season beef with salt and pepper, then brown in the bacon fat. Remove and set aside.
3. In the same pot, sauté onions, garlic, carrots, and celery until softened.
4. Add tomato paste and cook for a few minutes.
5. Return beef and bacon to the pot. Pour in red wine and beef broth. Add the bouquet garni.
6. Cover and simmer for about 2-3 hours until the beef is tender.

7. In a separate pan, melt butter and sauté pearl onions and mushrooms until browned.
8. Sprinkle flour over the mushroom mixture, stirring to create a roux.
9. Add the mushroom mixture to the beef, cooking for an additional 15-20 minutes.
10. Adjust seasoning and serve hot.

Estimated Total Time: Approximately 3-4 hours

## Lobster Bisque

A luxurious soup made with lobster meat and stock, requiring careful preparation and attention to detail.

Ingredients:

- 2 lobster tails
- 2 tablespoons unsalted butter
- 1 onion, chopped
- 2 carrots, chopped
- 2 celery stalks, chopped
- 2 cloves garlic, minced
- 1/4 cup brandy (optional)
- 4 cups seafood or chicken broth
- 1 cup heavy cream
- 2 tablespoons tomato paste
- 1 bay leaf
- Salt and pepper to taste
- Fresh chives for garnish (optional)

Preparation:

1. Steam or boil lobster tails until they turn red, then remove the meat from the shells and chop it into bite-sized pieces. Reserve the shells.
2. In a large pot, melt butter and sauté onions, carrots, celery, and garlic until softened.
3. If using, add brandy and cook for a few minutes.

4. Add lobster shells, seafood or chicken broth, heavy cream, tomato paste, and bay leaf to the pot.
5. Simmer for about 30-40 minutes.
6. Remove and discard the bay leaf and lobster shells.
7. Use an immersion blender to puree the soup until smooth. Alternatively, transfer to a blender in batches.
8. Return the soup to the pot, add lobster meat, and gently reheat.
9. Season with salt and pepper, garnish with fresh chives, and serve hot.

Estimated Total Time: Approximately 1 hour

### **Advanced Gourmet Recipes:

These advanced gourmet recipes offer exceptional flavours and presentation, making them perfect for special occasions and experienced cooks who want to take their culinary skills to the next level.

### Foie Gras with Port Wine Reduction

An upscale dish featuring seared foie gras with a complex port wine reduction sauce.

Ingredients:
- 4 foie gras slices (about 2-3 ounces each)
- 1 cup port wine
- 1/4 cup red wine vinegar
- 2 tablespoons granulated sugar
- Salt and pepper to taste

Preparation:

1. Score the foie gras slices with a crosshatch pattern and season them with salt and pepper.
2. In a saucepan, combine port wine, red wine vinegar, and granulated sugar. Bring to a simmer.
3. Reduce heat and let the mixture simmer gently until it thickens and reduces by about half (this can take 20-30 minutes). It should have a syrupy consistency.

4. Heat a skillet over medium-high heat. Place foie gras slices in the skillet.
5. Sear for about 1-2 minutes per side until they are browned on the outside but still pink inside.
6. Serve the foie gras with the port wine reduction sauce drizzled on top.

Estimated Total Time: Approximately 30-40 minutes

## Beef Wellington

A British masterpiece, this dish involves wrapping beef fillets in puff pastry with a mushroom duxelles.

Ingredients:
- 4 beef fillet steaks (about 6 ounces each)
- 4 slices of Parma ham
- 8-10 cremini mushrooms, finely chopped
- 2 cloves of garlic, minced
- 1 package of puff pastry
- Dijon mustard
- Egg wash (1 beaten egg)
- Salt and pepper to taste

Preparation:

1. Sear the beef fillets in a hot pan until browned on all sides. Set aside to cool.
2. In the same pan, sauté the minced garlic and chopped mushrooms until they release their moisture and the mixture thickens. Season with salt and pepper.
3. Spread a thin layer of Dijon mustard on each steak, then wrap them in Parma ham.
4. Roll out the puff pastry and cut into rectangles large enough to wrap each steak.
5. Place the mushroom mixture on the pastry, then the steak wrapped in ham.
6. Fold the pastry over the steak, sealing the edges with egg wash.
7. Brush the top with egg wash for a golden finish.
8. Bake at 400°F (200°C) for about 20-25 minutes until the pastry is golden brown and the beef is cooked to your liking.

Estimated Total Time: Approximately 1 hour

## Creme Brulee

A delicate French dessert with a caramelised sugar top, known for its precision in both cooking and presentation.

Ingredients:

- 6 large egg yolks
- 1/2 cup granulated sugar
- 2 cups heavy cream
- 1 vanilla bean or 1 teaspoon vanilla extract
- Granulated sugar (for caramelising)

Preparation:

1. Preheat your oven to 325°F (160°C).
2. In a saucepan, heat the heavy cream and vanilla bean (split and scraped) until it simmers. Remove from heat and let it steep for 10-15 minutes.
3. In a separate bowl, whisk egg yolks and granulated sugar until thick and pale.
4. Gradually add the hot cream mixture to the egg yolk mixture while whisking continuously.
5. Remove the vanilla bean if used and strain the mixture.
6. Pour the custard into ramekins.
7. Place the ramekins in a baking dish and fill the dish with hot water halfway up the sides of the ramekins.
8. Bake in the preheated oven for 30-40 minutes until the custard is set but still slightly jiggly in the centre.
9. Chill the custards in the refrigerator for at least 4 hours or overnight.
10. Before serving, sprinkle a thin, even layer of granulated sugar on top of each custard and caramelise it using a kitchen torch or under a broiler.

Estimated Total Time: Approximately 4-5 hours (including chilling time)

# **Conclusion**

Ah, my dear epicurean explorer, let us embark upon a journey to unveil the sublime secrets of culinary mastery!

With the grace of a swan and the wit of a raconteur, we shall traverse the delectable landscapes of gastronomic artistry, where flavours dance upon the palate like celestial constellations.

In the realm of haute cuisine, one must don the apron of audacity, the toque of tenacity, and the oven mitts of opulence.

The art of cooking, my dear reader, is nothing short of a symphony, where ingredients are the virtuosos and the chef, the maestro.

As we embark upon this delightful odyssey, let us not forget that the kitchen is a stage, and every dish a performance.

In this theatre of the senses, we must wield our spatulas like swords and our sauté pans like shields, for in the crucible of the kitchen, battles are won not with brute force, but with finesse and flavour.

Picture, if you will, a soirée of sauces, a cavalcade of casseroles, and a parade of pastries—all orchestrated with the precision of a Swiss watch.

Ah, the joy of creating, the thrill of experimenting, and the triumph of a perfectly executed béarnaise sauce!

But fear not, for even in the grandest of kitchens, mishaps are as common as a cheeky butler's wink. A soufflé may fall, a sauce may break, and a roast may resemble a charcoal briquette. Yet, it is in these moments of culinary calamity that we discover our true mettle.

For, my dear gastronome, the path to gourmet mastery is paved with delicious blunders.

And so, as we conclude this exploration of the culinary realm, remember this: In the grand banquet of life, let us savour each dish with mirth, for it is not only about the destination but also about the delightful detours along the way.

Bon appétit! Busy Professional!

## **Culinary Glossary**

**À la Carte**: Ordering individual dishes from a menu, as opposed to a fixed-price or set menu.

**Amuse-Bouche:** A small, complimentary appetiser served before a meal to excite the palate.

**Bearnaise:** A richland creamy sauce made with clarified butter, egg yolks, white wine and herbs , often served with steak or fish.

**Bouillabaisse**: A Provençal fish stew made with various fish and shellfish.Coulis: A thin sauce or puree made from fruits, vegetables, or herbs, often used as a garnish.

**Ceviche**: A Latin American dish made from fresh, raw fish or seafood marinated in citrus juice, often garnished with vegetables and herbs.

**Charcuterie:** A selection of cured meats, pâtés, terrines, and other prepared meat products, often served as an appetiser or on a platter

**Consomme:** A clear, flavourful broth made by clarifying stock with egg whites and other ingredients, often served as a soup.

**Creme Brulee:** A dessert made with rich custard topped with a layer of caramelised sugar, creating a crispy crust.

**Croquembouche:** A French dessert consisting of cream puffs, piled into a tower and bound together with caramelised sugar, often served at special occasions.

**Degustation**: A tasting menu featuring a sequence of small, carefully crafted dishes.

**Escoffier**: Auguste Escoffier, a legendary French chef known for his culinary contributions.

**Fillet:** The process of removing bones or skin from meat or fish.

**Foie Gras**: A luxury food product made from the fattened liver of a duck or goose, often served as a pate or in a whole lobe form.

**Gastrique**: A sweet and sour sauce made by caramelising sugar and deglazing it with vinegar, often used to add flavour to dishes

**Haute Cuisine**: High-quality, elaborate French cuisine associated with fine dining.Infusion: Extracting flavours by steeping ingredients in hot liquid.

**Jus**: A rich and concentrated meat or vegetable sauce, often served with roasted meats.

**Lardons**: Small strips of bacon or salt pork used for flavour and texture.

**Mirepoix**: A mixture of diced onions, carrots, and celery, used as a base for many sauces, soups, and stews.

**Molecular Gastronomy**: A culinary discipline exploring the science of cooking.

**Nouvelle Cuisine**: A French culinary movement featuring lighter, innovative dishes.

**Omakase**: A Japanese dining style where the chef creates a personalised tasting menu.

**Paillard**: Meat pounded thin for quick cooking or grilling.

**Panna Cotta**: An Italian dessert made with sweetened cream, often set with gelatin and served chilled

**Quenelle**: A dumpling-like shape made from a mixture of meat, fish, or vegetables.

**Reduction**: Simmering a liquid to concentrate flavours and thicken consistency.

**Ratatouille**: A Provencal vegetable stew made with a variety of ingredients such as eggplant, zucchini, tomatoes, and bell peppers

**Sous-Vide**: Cooking food in a vacuum-sealed bag at precise temperatures. A cooking technique where food is vacuum-sealed in a plastic pouch and cooked at a precise, low temperature in a water bath, resulting in tender and evenly cooked dishes

**Tartare**: A dish made of finely chopped raw meat or fish.

**Tiramisu**: An Italian dessert made with layers of coffee-soaked ladyfingers and mascarpone cheese, dusted with cocoa powder.

**Tranche**: A French term for a slice or portion of meat, often used in fine dining.

**Truffle**: An expensive and highly prized mushroom variety often used to infuse dishes with a unique and intense flavour.

**Umami**: The fifth basic taste, savoury and often associated with ingredients like soy sauce.

**Velouté**: A classic French sauce made with a roux (butter and flour) and a light stock, often used as a base for other sauces.

**Vichyssoise**: A chilled potato and leek soup.

**Wagyu**: A highly prized and marbled breed of Japanese beef.

**Xiaolongbao**: Chinese steamed dumplings with meat and flavorful broth.

**Yuzu**: A Japanese citrus fruit known for its tangy flavour

**Zest**: The aromatic rind of citrus fruits used to add flavour.

# Recommended Resources for Gourmet Fine Dining

Here's a Selection of Resources across various aspects of Gourmet and Fine Dining:

### *Books:

"Eleven Madison Park: The Cookbook" by Daniel Humm and Will Guidara: Offers a glimpse into the culinary artistry of the renowned Eleven Madison Park restaurant.

"Essentials of Classic Italian Cooking" by Marcella Hazan: A classic cookbook that delves into the heart of Italian cuisine, with traditional recipes and expert guidance.

"French Laundry Cookbook" by Thomas Keller: Offers insights into the world of French haute cuisine from the acclaimed chef of The French Laundry.

"Larousse Gastronomique": Often referred to as the "culinary bible," this comprehensive encyclopaedia covers a wide range of culinary topics, techniques, and recipes.

"Modernist Cuisine: The Art and Science of Cooking" by Nathan Myhrvold, Chris Young, and Maxime Bilet: A groundbreaking multi-volume work that explores the science and techniques behind modern cuisine.

"Noma: Time and Place in Nordic Cuisine" by René Redzepi: Chronicles the culinary journey of Noma, one of the world's most innovative restaurants, and its emphasis on Nordic cuisine.

"Sous-Vide at Home: The Modern Technique for Perfectly Cooked Meals" by Lisa Q. Fetterman: A guide to sous-vide cooking techniques, enabling readers to create gourmet meals at home.

"The Art of Fermentation" by Sandor Ellix Katz: An exploration of the world of fermentation, offering insights into making a variety of gourmet fermented foods.

"The Flavor Bible" by Karen Page and Andrew Dornenburg: An essential reference guide for chefs and food enthusiasts, offering insights into flavour pairings and creative culinary combinations.

"The French Laundry Cookbook" by Thomas Keller: A beautifully crafted cookbook featuring recipes and insights from one of the world's most acclaimed chefs.

"The Professional Chef" by The Culinary Institute of America: A foundational textbook for culinary professionals, covering a wide range of techniques and concepts.

### *Cooking Classes and Workshops:

America's Test Kitchen Cooking School: Website: www.cookschool.athome.com
Offers an array of cooking courses and tutorials, with a strong emphasis on the science behind cooking techniques.

ChefSteps: Website: www.chefsteps.com
Known for their modernist and innovative approach to cooking, ChefSteps offers online classes and recipes for those looking to push culinary boundaries.

Culinary Institute of America (CIA): Website: www.ciachef.edu
CIA is one of the most renowned culinary schools in the world. They offer a variety of programs, including online classes, for both amateurs and professionals.

Le Cordon Bleu: Website: www.cordonbleu.edu
Known for its classical culinary training, Le Cordon Bleu offers online courses and workshops covering various cuisines and techniques.

MasterClass: Website: www.masterclass.com
MasterClass offers celebrity-led cooking classes. Learn from culinary icons like Gordon Ramsay, Thomas Keller, and Massimo Bottura.

Rouxbe: Website: www.rouxbe.com

Rouxbe is an online culinary school with interactive cooking courses and a focus on professional-level training.

## *Cooking Equipment and Tools:

Amazon: Website: www.amazon.com
Amazon offers a vast selection of kitchen equipment and tools from various brands and price ranges. You can read customer reviews and compare products easily.

Williams Sonoma: Website: www.williams-sonoma.com
Williams Sonoma is known for its high-quality cookware, bakeware, and kitchen gadgets. They also have a range of gourmet food products.

Sur La Table: Website: www.surlatable.com
Sur La Table offers a wide range of kitchen tools and equipment, along with cooking classes and workshops.

Bed Bath & Beyond: Website: www.bedbathandbeyond.com
This store offers an extensive selection of kitchen essentials, including cookware, small appliances, and utensils.

Crate & Barrel: Website: www.crateandbarrel.com
Crate & Barrel offers stylish and functional kitchen tools, cookware, and bakeware.

Chef's Catalog: Website: www.chefscatalog.com
A specialised kitchen supply store with a focus on professional-grade equipment and tools.

KitchenAid: Website: www.kitchenaid.com
If you're looking for high-quality kitchen appliances, especially stand mixers and attachments, KitchenAid is a reputable choice.

Cutlery and More: Website: www.cutleryandmore.com
This store specialises in cutlery and knives, offering a wide range of options for chefs at all levels.

The Cook's Warehouse: Website: www.cookswarehouse.com

A kitchen supply store that offers a curated selection of high-quality cookware, bakeware, and culinary tools.

WebstaurantStore: Website: www.webstaurantstore.com

This online store caters to both home chefs and professional kitchens, offering a wide range of restaurant-grade equipment and supplies.

All-Clad: Website: www.all-clad.com

If you're looking for premium cookware and kitchen essentials, All-Clad is known for its high-quality stainless steel products.

Zwilling J.A. Henckels: Website: www.zwilling.com

Renowned for their cutlery and kitchenware, Zwilling J.A. Henckels offers top-notch knives and cookware.

## *Culinary Apps:

### Gourmet Recipes Apps:

Yummly:
- Available for both iOS and Android.
- Offers a vast collection of recipes, personalized recommendations, and shopping lists.

Tasty:
- Available for both iOS and Android.
- Features step-by-step video recipes and a variety of gourmet dishes.

Epicurious:
- Available for both iOS and Android.
- Offers a vast library of gourmet recipes, cooking tips, and the ability to create shopping lists.

Cookpad:
- Available for both iOS and Android.

- A community-driven app where users share their favourite gourmet recipes.

Food Network Kitchen:
- Available for both iOS and Android.
- Provides access to Food Network's library of gourmet recipes and cooking classes.

*Wine Pairing Apps:*

Vivino:
- Available for both iOS and Android.
- Helps you find and purchase wines, as well as offers wine pairing suggestions for various dishes.

Wine Spectator WineRatings+:
- Available for both iOS and Android.
- Provides wine ratings, reviews, and wine-pairing recommendations from Wine Spectator.

Delectable:
- Available for both iOS and Android.
- Offers wine label recognition, reviews, and personalized wine recommendations.

*Restaurant Reviews and Reservations Apps:*

OpenTable:
- Available for both iOS and Android.
- Allows users to make restaurant reservations and read reviews from other diners.

Yelp:
- Available for both iOS and Android.
- Provides restaurant reviews, ratings, and photos from users, helping you discover new gourmet dining options.

TripAdvisor:
- Available for both iOS and Android.
- Offers restaurant reviews, ratings, and travel-related information for gourmet dining experiences.

Zomato:
- Available for both iOS and Android.
- Provides restaurant reviews, ratings, and menus for a wide range of dining establishments.

Resy:
- Available for both iOS and Android.
- Focuses on helping users discover and make reservations at top restaurants in various cities.

## *Culinary Documentaries and Films:

Documentaries:

Jiro Dreams of Sushi (2011):
- Director: David Gelb
- This documentary profiles Jiro Ono, an 85-year-old sushi master in Tokyo, and his dedication to perfecting the art of sushi.

Chef's Table (2015-2018):
- A Netflix documentary series that features in-depth profiles of world-renowned chefs and their culinary journeys.

Barbecue (2017):
- Director: Matthew Salleh
- Explores the global tradition of barbecue and the cultural significance of this cooking method.

Somm (2012):
- Director: Jason Wise
- Follows four candidates as they prepare for the Master Sommelier exam, delving into the world of wine.

Jeremiah Tower: The Last Magnificent (2016):
- Director: Lydia Tenaglia
- Chronicles the life and career of renowned American chef Jeremiah Tower, a pioneer of California cuisine.

The Birth of Sake (2015):
- Director: Erik Shirai
- Offers an inside look at the art of sake brewing in a traditional Japanese brewery.

For Grace (2015):
- Directors: Kevin Pang and Mark Helenowski
- Follows the journey of Chef Curtis Duffy as he strives to open his own restaurant, Grace, in Chicago.

Narrative Films:

Julie & Julia (2009):
- Director: Nora Ephron
- Based on the true story of Julie Powell, who decides to cook her way through Julia Child's cookbook, "Mastering the Art of French Cooking."

Ratatouille (2007):
- Director: Brad Bird
- An animated film that tells the story of a rat with a passion for cooking who befriends a young chef in Paris.

Burnt (2015):
- Director: John Wells
- Features Bradley Cooper as a talented but troubled chef striving for culinary greatness.

Haute Cuisine (2012):
- Directors: Christian Vincent

- Inspired by the true story of Danièle Delpeuch, the personal chef to French President François Mitterrand.

The Hundred-Foot Journey (2014):
- Director: Lasse Hallström
- Follows the journey of an Indian family who opens a restaurant in France, leading to a culinary clash and eventual fusion.

### *Food and Cooking Communities:

*Online Forums:*

eGullet (www.egullet.org):
- eGullet is a long-established online community dedicated to food and drink. It features discussions on various culinary topics, from recipes to restaurant reviews.

ChefTalk (www.cheftalk.com):
- A forum for both professional chefs and home cooks, ChefTalk offers a place to discuss recipes, techniques, and all things food-related.

Food52 Community (community.food52.com):
- Food52's community forum allows members to share recipes, cooking advice, and kitchen tips.

Chowhound (www.chowhound.com):
- Chowhound has regional boards where members discuss local restaurants, food trends, and cooking tips.

*Social Media Groups:*

Reddit - r/Cooking (www.reddit.com/r/Cooking):
- Reddit's r/Cooking community is a popular place to ask questions, share recipes, and participate in discussions about cooking.

Reddit - r/Food (www.reddit.com/r/food):

- The r/Food subreddit is dedicated to sharing food-related content, including recipes, food photos, and cooking experiences.

*Facebook Groups:*

- Facebook hosts various cooking and food-related groups. Search for groups related to your interests, such as "Home Cooking Enthusiasts" or "Foodie Adventures."

*Instagram:*

- Follow gourmet chefs, food bloggers, and enthusiasts on Instagram. Use hashtags like #foodie, #gourmet, and #cooking to discover like-minded individuals.

*Specialised Communities:*

- Baking Bites Forum (forum.baking911.com):
- A community specifically focused on baking, where members discuss bread, cakes, cookies, and more.

*The Fresh Loaf (www.thefreshloaf.com):*

- A community for bread enthusiasts, offering discussions on bread recipes, techniques, and troubleshooting.

*Cheese.com Community (www.cheese.com/community):*

- If you're passionate about cheese, this community allows you to connect with fellow cheese lovers, share tasting notes, and learn more about cheese.

*Wine Spectator Forums (forums.winespectator.com):*

- Wine enthusiasts can participate in discussions about wine, winemaking, and wine-related travel.

### *Food and Wine Tours:

Epicurean Ways (www.epicureanways.com):

- Epicurean Ways specializes in food and wine tours to Spain, Portugal, and Argentina, offering guided culinary experiences and visits to wineries.

Zicasso (www.zicasso.com):

- Zicasso offers customized food and wine tours to destinations around the world. They connect travelers with expert travel planners to create unique gourmet experiences.

Wine Paths (www.winepaths.com):

- Wine Paths provides luxury wine and culinary tours to various wine regions, including France, Italy, and South Africa.

Food & Wine Trails (www.foodandwinetrails.com):

- Specialising in wine cruises and tours, Food & Wine Trails offers a range of culinary and wine-focused travel experiences.

Culinary Backstreets (www.culinarybackstreets.com):

- Culinary Backstreets offers food tours in cities around the world, providing a deep dive into local food traditions and hidden culinary gems.

Gourmet Getaways (www.gourmetgetaways.com):

- Gourmet Getaways offers food and wine tours in Australia and New Zealand, focusing on the region's culinary delights.

International Culinary Tours (www.internationalculinarytours.com):

- This company offers culinary vacations to destinations such as France, Italy, and Thailand, where travelers can learn from local chefs and explore food markets.

Experi (www.experi.com):

- Experi specializes in immersive culinary tours and cooking classes in various countries, including Japan, Mexico, and Morocco.

Wine Country Getaways (www.winecountrygetaways.com):

- Wine Country Getaways focuses on wine-centric tours in regions like Napa Valley, Sonoma County, and other renowned wine destinations in the United States.

Gourmet On Tour (www.gourmetontour.com):

- Gourmet On Tour offers food and wine tours throughout Europe, with a focus on culinary experiences and wine tastings.

Gastronomad Experiences (www.gastronomad.net):

- Gastronomad Experiences offers unique, small-group culinary adventures in destinations around the world.

Backroads (www.backroads.com):

- While primarily known for biking and hiking tours, Backroads also offers active culinary adventures in various regions.

*Gourmet Food Festivals and Events

South Beach Wine & Food Festival (SOBEWFF):

- Location: Miami Beach, Florida, USA

- This festival, hosted by the Food Network & Cooking Channel, features celebrity chefs, wine tastings, and food seminars.

### Aspen Food & Wine Classic:

- Location: Aspen, Colorado, USA
- A renowned event that brings together celebrity chefs, winemakers, and food enthusiasts for a weekend of tastings, cooking demonstrations, and panel discussions.

### Taste of Chicago:

- Location: Chicago, Illinois, USA
- One of the largest food festivals in the world, featuring a wide variety of cuisine from local restaurants and food vendors.

### Pebble Beach Food & Wine:

- Location: Pebble Beach, California, USA
- This event offers wine tastings, cooking demos, and gourmet dinners prepared by world-famous chefs.

### New York City Wine & Food Festival (NYCWFF):

- Location: New York City, New York, USA
- NYCWFF showcases culinary talent from around the world, including celebrity chefs, food tastings, and cooking classes.

### Austin Food + Wine Festival:

- Location: Austin, Texas, USA
- A celebration of food and wine featuring local and national chefs, cooking demos, and live music.

### Chicago Gourmet:

- Location: Chicago, Illinois, USA
- A food and wine festival highlighting the city's top restaurants and chefs, with tastings, seminars, and culinary demonstrations.

### The Big Feastival:
- Location: Various locations, including the UK and Canada
- A family-friendly food and music festival featuring celebrity chefs, artisanal food vendors, and live music performances.

### Feast Portland:
- Location: Portland, Oregon, USA
- A celebration of Pacific Northwest cuisine with food tastings, culinary events, and collaborations with local and national chefs.

### San Francisco Street Food Festival:
- Location: San Francisco, California, USA
- A gathering of food trucks and vendors serving a diverse array of international street foods.

### The Melbourne Food and Wine Festival:
- Location: Melbourne, Australia
- Australia's premier food and wine event featuring cooking demonstrations, wine tastings, and special dining experiences.

### Taste of London: -
- Location: London, UK
- A food festival showcasing the city's top restaurants and chefs, with tastings, masterclasses, and live cooking demonstrations.

### Savour Singapore:
- Location: Singapore
- An epicurean festival featuring top chefs, gourmet dining experiences, and culinary workshops.

***Magazines and Food Publications:**

Food & Wine: This magazine covers a wide range of topics related to food, wine, and fine dining.

Bon Appétit: Known for its in-depth features on gourmet cuisine and recipes from renowned chefs.

Gourmet Traveller: This publication focuses on gourmet travel experiences and fine dining around the world.

Saveur: A magazine that explores global cuisine, traditional recipes, and culinary traditions.

Epicurious: While primarily a digital platform, Epicurious offers a wealth of gourmet recipes and food-related content.

Fine Cooking: This magazine is dedicated to providing recipes, tips, and techniques for home cooks looking to create gourmet dishes.

Cuisine at Home: Offers easy-to-follow recipes and techniques for gourmet home cooking.

Art Culinaire: Known for its stunning food photography and in-depth exploration of gourmet dishes.

Wine Spectator: While wine-focused, this publication often features articles on pairing wine with gourmet food.

Gastronomica: A scholarly journal that delves into the cultural and historical aspects of food and fine dining.

***Online Blogs**

David Lebovitz (davidlebovitz.com): David Lebovitz is a pastry chef, author, and food blogger known for his delectable dessert recipes and insights into Parisian dining.

Smitten Kitchen (smittenkitchen.com): Deb Perelman's blog features approachable gourmet recipes, stunning food photography, and delightful anecdotes.

The Kitchn (thekitchn.com): A comprehensive food and cooking blog with a variety of gourmet recipes, cooking tips, and kitchen hacks

101 Cookbooks (101cookbooks.com): Heidi Swanson's blog focuses on whole, natural foods and features gourmet vegetarian recipes inspired by her travels.

Lottie + Doof (lottieanddoof.com): A beautifully designed blog featuring gourmet recipes, restaurant recommendations, and thoughtful food writing.

The Woks of Life (thewoksoflife.com): A family-run blog offering gourmet Asian recipes, cooking tutorials, and cultural insights.

Half Baked Harvest (halfbakedharvest.com): Tieghan Gerard's blog features gourmet comfort food recipes and stunning food photography.

I Am a Food Blog (iamafoodblog.com): A blog with a focus on modern and creative gourmet recipes, often with a unique twist.

Lady and Pups (ladyandpups.com): Mandy Lee's blog combines stunning food photography with gourmet recipes that often have an Asian-inspired flair.

The Little Kitchen (thelittlekitchen.net): Features gourmet recipes, travel-inspired dishes, and entertaining tips.

Rasa Malaysia (rasamalaysia.com): Specialises in gourmet Malaysian recipes, offering a taste of authentic Malaysian cuisine.

Eat the Love (eatthelove.com): A blog with gourmet dessert recipes and thoughtful reflections on the art of baking.

Green Kitchen Stories (greenkitchenstories.com): Focuses on vegetarian and plant-based gourmet recipes with a Scandinavian twist.

The Bojon Gourmet (bojongourmet.com): Alanna Taylor-Tobin's blog offers stunning gluten-free gourmet recipes and photography.

No Recipes (norecipes.com): Marc Matsumoto's blog explores gourmet recipes inspired by Japanese and international cuisines.

## *Online Cooking Classes:

MasterClass: Offers courses by world-renowned chefs, including Gordon Ramsay, Thomas Keller, and Massimo Bottura.

Rouxbe: Provides online culinary education and cooking classes suitable for both beginners and experienced cooks.

The Culinary Institute of America (CIA): The CIA offers online cooking courses that cover various aspects of gourmet cooking and fine dining.

Udemy: Udemy has a variety of cooking courses, including gourmet and fine dining options, often taught by experienced chefs.

America's Test Kitchen Online Cooking School: Known for its meticulous recipe testing, America's Test Kitchen offers online courses that can help you master gourmet cooking.

Le Cordon Bleu Online Learning: Le Cordon Bleu offers online courses that allow you to learn classic and gourmet cooking techniques.

ChefSteps: ChefSteps focuses on modern cooking techniques and offers online classes that can help you create gourmet dishes with a modern twist.

Sur La Table Online Cooking Classes: Sur La Table offers a variety of online cooking classes, including some focused on gourmet cuisine.

## *Podcasts:

Gastropod: This podcast explores the science and history behind food and culinary traditions, often delving into gourmet and fine dining topics.

The Sporkful: While not exclusively focused on fine dining, The Sporkful podcast discusses food culture, etiquette, and the art of eating, often featuring guests from the world of gourmet cuisine.

The Fine Dining Podcast: This podcast is dedicated to exploring the world of fine dining, featuring interviews with chefs, sommeliers, and industry insiders.

The Mitchen: Hosted by some of Australia's top chefs and food writers, The Mitchen dives into the world of food, including gourmet dining experiences.

Burnt Toast: This podcast covers a wide range of food-related topics, including gourmet cooking, culinary history, and food trends.

The Eater Upsell: From Eater.com, this podcast discusses food and dining culture, occasionally featuring insights into gourmet dining experiences.

Home Cooking: Hosted by Samin Nosrat and Hrishikesh Hirway, this podcast explores various aspects of cooking and occasionally touches on gourmet techniques and recipes.

Radio Cherry Bombe: While mainly focusing on women in the food industry, this podcast often features conversations with chefs and entrepreneurs in the gourmet food world..

## *Professional Associations:

American Culinary Federation (ACF): ACF provides certification, educational resources, and networking opportunities for culinary professionals.

James Beard Foundation: This organization celebrates and supports chefs and the food industry through scholarships, awards, and culinary events.

Les Dames d'Escoffier International: An invitation-only organization for women in the culinary, beverage, and hospitality industries that offers mentorship and networking.

Chaine des Rotisseurs: A gastronomic society focused on fine dining and culinary excellence, with events and competitions.

World Association of Chefs' Societies (Worldchefs): It's a global network of chefs' associations, offering training, competitions, and international culinary connections.

Institute of Culinary Education (ICE): While not an association, ICE is a culinary school that offers classes, programs, and resources for aspiring chefs.

International Association of Culinary Professionals (IACP): IACP connects culinary professionals, offering resources, conferences, and publications.

Society of Wine Educators: For those interested in the wine and beverage side of gourmet dining, this organization provides education and certification.

Slow Food International: Focused on promoting sustainable and local food, Slow Food offers educational programs and events for food enthusiasts.

### *Specialty Food Suppliers:

Specialty Food Stores: Look for local specialty food stores or gourmet markets in your area. These often carry a wide range of unique ingredients, artisanal products, and high-quality kitchen equipment.

Online Retailers: There are numerous online retailers that specialize in gourmet and specialty food products. Websites like Amazon, Food52, and Williams-Sonoma offer a vast selection of ingredients and kitchen equipment.

Farmers' Markets: Farmers' markets can be great sources for fresh, locally-produced specialty ingredients and artisanal products. Many vendors at these markets offer unique and seasonal items.

Cheesemongers: If you're looking for specialty cheeses, visit a local cheesemonger or a cheese shop. They often carry a variety of artisanal cheeses from around the world.

Butcher Shops: Specialty butcher shops can provide high-quality cuts of meat and unique sausages or charcuterie items that may not be readily available in standard grocery stores.

Asian, Ethnic, or International Markets: These markets are excellent for finding specialty ingredients from different cuisines around the world. You can discover unique spices, sauces, and ingredients specific to various regions.

Online Specialty Food Retailers: Explore online specialty food retailers like iGourmet, Dean & DeLuca, or Gustiamo, which offer a curated selection of gourmet products.

Kitchen Supply Stores: Stores like Sur La Table and Bed Bath & Beyond have sections dedicated to gourmet kitchen equipment and tools, including cookware, bakeware, and gadgets.

Artisanal Producers: Many small-scale, artisanal producers sell their products directly to consumers through their websites or at local food festivals and events. This is an excellent way to discover unique and handcrafted items.

Wine and Spirits Shops: These stores often carry specialty wines, spirits, and cocktail ingredients that can enhance your culinary creations..

## *Wine and Beverage Resources:

### Wine Education:

Wine Folly: Wine Folly is an excellent website and book series that provides accessible and visual wine education. They offer articles, videos, and infographics on wine regions, grape varieties, and wine tasting techniques.

Wine Spectator: Wine Spectator's website and magazine offer in-depth wine reviews, ratings, and educational content, including wine basics and wine-pairing guides.

GuildSomm: GuildSomm is a valuable resource for wine professionals and enthusiasts. They provide educational materials, articles, and forums for wine knowledge sharing.

Sommelier Courses: Consider enrolling in sommelier courses or wine education programs, such as those offered by the Court of Master Sommeliers or the Wine & Spirit Education Trust (WSET).

## Cocktail Recipes:

Difford's Guide: Difford's Guide is a comprehensive resource for cocktail recipes and mixology knowledge. They offer a vast collection of cocktail recipes, including classics and innovative creations.

Cocktail Books: Explore cocktail recipe books written by renowned mixologists, such as "The Joy of Mixology" by Gary Regan or "The Craft of the Cocktail" by Dale DeGroff.

Online Cocktail Communities: Join online cocktail enthusiast communities or forums where members share their favorite cocktail recipes and tips. Websites like Liquor.com and Cocktail Chemistry's YouTube channel are also great resources.

## Beverage Pairings:

James Beard Foundation: The James Beard Foundation offers resources and articles on food and beverage pairings, including wine, beer, and spirits, to enhance your dining experience.

Craft Beer and Spirits Guides: If you're interested in beer or spirits pairings, explore resources from craft breweries and distilleries. They often provide pairing suggestions for their products on their websites.

Local Wine Tasting Events: Attend local wine tasting events and festivals to learn about regional wine pairings and discover new favourites.

Wine and Food Pairing Apps: There are smartphone apps that can suggest wine pairings based on the dishes you plan to prepare or order. Examples include Vivino and Wine Spectator's WineRatings+.

## Afterword: Reflecting on Gourmet Dining

Ah, my dear reader, we have embarked on a gastronomic journey so exquisite, even the finest wines would blush with envy.

As I sit here, surrounded by the remnants of a culinary odyssey, allow me to share a few reflections on our gourmet escapade.

Firstly, one must admit, indulging in the world of gourmet dining does wonders for the soul. It's akin to a symphony of flavours that dances upon the palate like a group of tango aficionados, leaving you breathless and longing for an encore.

Ah, the truffle! That subterranean jewel of the culinary world. It's as if Mother Nature herself decided to hide her treasures underground, just to test our determination.

We, my dear reader, have proven ourselves worthy in our pursuit of these delectable fungi.

And then, the art of pairing wine with food – a task not for the faint of heart! Selecting the perfect vintage to accompany a dish is like choosing the right accessory for an haute couture gown. The wrong choice, and disaster looms. But the right pairing? Pure magic!

Let us not forget the delightful chefs who toil away in their kitchens, their passion and creativity giving birth to edible masterpieces. They are the unsung heroes of our gourmet adventure, creating symphonies of flavours that transport us to culinary nirvana.

In closing, my fellow connoisseur of the culinary arts, remember that gourmet dining is not just about sustenance; it's a celebration of life itself.

So, as you sip your champagne and savour the last crumbs of that decadent dessert, know that you have dined as royalty, even if it was just in spirit.

Until we meet again at the table of epicurean delights, raise your fork high, my dear reader, and toast to a life deliciously lived.

Yours gastronomically,

Casimir Thistledown

Printed in Great Britain
by Amazon